What one loves in childhood,
stays in the heart forever.
-Mary Jo Putney

## Baked Macaroni & Cheese

1 c. elbow macaroni, cooked
   and drained
1 c. soft bread crumbs
1 t. onion, chopped
1 c. Cheddar cheese, grated

1-1/2 c. milk
2 eggs, beaten
1 T. butter
salt, pepper and paprika to
   taste

Combine all ingredients well. Spoon into a well greased
one-quart baking dish. Bake, uncovered, at 375 degrees for
45 minutes or until bubbly and golden. Makes 4 servings.

No matter where
I serve my guests
It seems they like
My kitchen best

Keep a stash of aprons in big and little sizes
so that everyone who wants to help
out in the kitchen, can!

## Golden Potato Bake

2 lbs. Yukon Gold potatoes,
    thinly sliced
1 onion, thinly sliced
1 red or yellow pepper, thinly
    sliced
1 T. chicken bouillon
    granules

1 T. Dijon mustard
1 t. dill weed
1 1/2 c. hot water
1/4 t. white pepper

Layer potatoes, onion and pepper slices in a lightly greased
2-quart baking dish; end with layer of potatoes. In a 2-cup
glass measure, stir together remaining ingredients; drizzle over
vegetables. Bake, covered, at 350 degrees for 45 minutes;
uncover and continue baking an additional 15 minutes or until
potatoes are tender. Makes 8 servings.

If you're taking a casserole to a potluck or picnic, keep
it toasty by covering the casserole
dish with foil then wrapping it in several
layers of newspaper.

## Crunchy Chicken Casserole

6-oz. pkg. wild rice, uncooked

14-1/2 oz. can French-style green beans, drained

10-3/4 oz. can cream of chicken soup

1/2 c. mayonnaise

4 skinless, boneless chicken breasts, cooked

8-oz. can water chestnuts, drained and sliced

1-oz. pkg. slivered almonds

2 c. shredded mild Cheddar cheese

Cook rice 5 minutes less than directed on package; mix with remaining ingredients except cheese. Pour into a greased 13"x9" baking dish; top with cheese. Bake, uncovered at 350 degrees for 30 minutes. Makes 4 servings.

For fluffy rice, cook covered (no peeking!) and don't stir while cooking.

# Green Beans Supreme

1 onion, sliced
1 T. fresh parsley, snipped
3 T. butter, divided
2 T. all-purpose flour
1/2 t. lemon zest
1/2 t. salt
1/8 t. pepper
1/2 c. milk
1 c. sour cream
2  9-oz. pkgs. frozen French-
    style green beans, cooked
1/2 c. shredded Cheddar
    cheese
1/4 c. bread crumbs

Cook onion and parsley in 2 tablespoons butter until onion is tender. Blend in flour, lemon zest, salt and pepper; add milk, stirring until thick and bubbly. Mix in sour cream and beans; heat through. Spoon into an ungreased 2-quart baking dish; sprinkle with cheese. Melt remaining butter and toss with bread crumbs; sprinkle on top of beans. Broil until golden. Makes 4 to 6 servings.

For a great flavor, squeeze fresh lemon juice on your
cooked veggies instead of salt.

## Make-Ahead Brunch Casserole

1 T. butter
2 onions, chopped
2 c. sliced mushrooms
4 c. frozen hash browns,
    thawed
salt & pepper to taste
1/4 t. garlic salt

1 lb. bacon, crisply cooked
    and crumbled
4 eggs
1-1/2 c. milk
1/8 t. dried parsley
1 c. shredded Cheddar cheese

In a medium skillet, melt butter and sauté onions and
mushrooms until tender. Place hash browns in the bottom of a
greased 13"x9" baking dish. Sprinkle with salt, pepper and
garlic salt. Top with bacon, onions and mushrooms. In a
medium mixing bowl, beat eggs with milk and parsley, pour
over casserole and top with cheese. Cover and refrigerate
overnight. Bake, uncovered, at 400 degrees for one hour or
until set. Makes 4 to 6 servings.

To keep bacon slices from sticking together,
roll the package into a tube shape and secure with
a rubber band before storing in the refrigerator.
Makes them so easy to use when you're ready!

# Hash Brown Potato Casserole

1 c. sour cream
2-lb. pkg. frozen hash
   browns
1/4 c. margarine
10-3/4 oz. can cream of
   mushroom soup

10-3/4 oz. can cream of
   chicken soup
2 c. Cheddar cheese, grated
1 c. corn flake cereal,
   crushed

Mix all ingredients together except corn flake cereal. Bake,
uncovered, in a 13"x9" baking pan at 375 degrees for
45 minutes. Cover top with crushed corn flake cereal and bake
an additional 15 minutes. Makes 12 to 15 servings.

What a time-saver! Prepare your casserole the night
before, cover and refrigerate. When
ready to make, just add 15 to
20 minutes to the cooking time.

## Apple & Sausage Stuffing

1 lb. sweet Italian sausage
1 onion, diced
2 stalks celery, chopped
1 apple, cored, peeled
   and diced
1 T. oil

2-1/2 c. water
1/2 c. margarine
16-oz. pkg. herb-seasoned
   stuffing mix
1 t. fennel seed

In a large skillet, brown sausage over medium heat; drain, let cool and crumble. Place onion, celery, apple and oil in skillet; sauté until tender. Remove from heat; set aside. Heat water and margarine in a saucepan to a boil; remove from heat. In a large mixing bowl, combine stuffing mix with water and margarine; toss lightly until moist throughout. Add fennel seed; blend well. Gently stir in onion mixture and sausage. Spoon stuffing in cavity of turkey or place in a 2-quart baking dish and bake, covered, at 350 degrees for 30 minutes. Serves 8 to 10.

*It is probably illegal to make soups, stews and casseroles without plenty of onions.*
*– Maggie Waldron*

## Sweet Potato Casserole

3 c. sweet potatoes, cooked
   and mashed
1 c. sugar
1/2 t. salt

2 eggs
2-1/2 T. margarine, melted
1/2 c. milk
1 t. vanilla extract

Mix all ingredients together and pour into a greased 2-quart
baking dish; sprinkle with topping. Bake, uncovered, at
350 degrees for 30 to 35 minutes or until brown sugar melts.
Makes 4 to 6 servings.

## Topping:

1 c. brown sugar, packed
1 c. chopped nuts

1/3 c. all-purpose flour
2-1/2 T. margarine, melted

Blend all ingredients together in a small bowl.

Keep a notepad taped to the inside of a kitchen cabinet
door... it's an easy way to keep a running grocery list as
you run out of items.

## Bravissimo Beefy Bake

2  11-oz. pkgs. frozen
   creamed chipped beef,
   thawed
1/2 c. frozen peas
2-1/2 oz. can sliced mushrooms, undrained
3 T. onion, chopped
1 t. Worcestershire sauce

1/4 t. pepper
3/4 c. biscuit baking mix
1 egg, beaten
1/2 c. milk
1/4 t. onion powder
1 c. shredded Cheddar
   cheese

Combine first 6 ingredients together, mixing well; transfer to
an ungreased 8"x8" baking dish. In a medium-size mixing
bowl, stir biscuit mix, egg, milk and onion powder together;
mix until smooth. Spoon over beef mixture; sprinkle with
cheese. Bake, uncovered, at 400 degrees for 30 to 35 minutes.
Makes 6 to 8 servings.

To shred cheese more easily, just
freeze it for 15 minutes.

# Tuna-Pea Wiggle

10-3/4 oz. can cream of
   celery soup
1/2 c. milk
2 c. egg noodles, cooked
2 6-oz. cans tuna, drained
   and flaked

1 c. frozen peas
2 T. dry bread crumbs
1 T. butter, melted

Combine soup and milk in a 1-1/2 quart baking dish; add
noodles, tuna and peas. Bake, covered, at 400 degrees for
20 minutes; stir. In a separate bowl, mix crumbs and butter;
sprinkle over casserole. Bake an additional 5 minutes.
Serves 4.

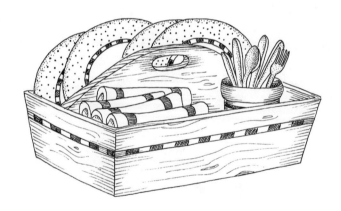

It's easy to separate frozen vegetables...put them in a
colander and pour on hot water. Let water drain into the
sink and add veggies to casserole ingredients.

# Classics

## Lasagna

1/2 lb. ground beef
1/2 lb. Italian sausage
1 clove garlic, minced
2 T. Italian seasoning
1-lb. can Italian stewed
  tomatoes
2  6-oz. cans tomato paste
1 onion, diced
2 eggs
3 c. ricotta cheese
1/2 c. grated Parmesan
  cheese
salt & pepper to taste
2 T. dried parsley flakes
10-oz. pkg. lasagna noodles,
  cooked
16-oz. pkg. shredded
  mozzarella cheese

Brown beef and sausage; drain. Add garlic, Italian seasoning, tomatoes, tomato paste and onion; simmer until onion is tender. In a large bowl, mix eggs, ricotta, Parmesan cheese, salt, pepper and parsley together; set aside. In a 13"x9" baking pan, layer noodles, cheese mixture, meat sauce, mozzarella cheese; repeat layers until pan is filled, being sure to end with mozzarella cheese. Cover with aluminum foil and bake at 350 degrees for 45 minutes to one hour. Makes 6 to 8 servings.

Hang a vintage chalkboard up in the kitchen and give family & friends a sneak peek at today's special!

# Virginia's Baked Spaghetti

16-oz. pkg. spaghetti
   noodles, cooked
2 24-oz. jars spaghetti sauce
2 lbs. ground beef, browned
4 T. butter
4 T. all-purpose flour
4 T. grated Parmesan cheese
2 t. salt
1/2 t. garlic powder
12-oz. can evaporated milk
3 c. shredded Cheddar
   cheese, divided

Combine spaghetti noodles, spaghetti sauce and ground beef;
set aside. In a saucepan, over medium heat, melt butter; add
flour, Parmesan cheese, salt and garlic. Stir constantly over
heat until smooth and bubbly. Add evaporated milk and one
cup Cheddar cheese; stir until thoroughly melted. Pour half of
the spaghetti noodle mixture into a 13"x9" casserole dish and
pour cheese mixture over the top. Pour remaining noodle
mixture into casserole dish; top with remaining Cheddar
cheese. Bake, uncovered, at 350 degrees for 25 to 30 minutes.
Makes 12 to 14 servings.

Celebrate Good Neighbor Day
on September 28th! Take a
homemade casserole (along
with the recipe!) and some
warm apple cider to
next-door
neighbors...toast to
your friendship.

## Shepherd's Pie

1 lb. ground beef
1/4 c. onion, chopped
1/2 t. salt
1-oz. pkg. brown gravy mix
10-oz. pkg. frozen peas and
   carrots

1/2 t. dried basil leaves
1/4 c. shredded Cheddar
   cheese
1-1/2 c. mashed potatoes,
   seasoned and warmed

Brown ground beef and onion over medium-high until onions
are tender; sprinkle with salt. Prepare gravy mix according to
package directions; add to meat mixture. After gravy thickens,
add frozen vegetables and basil; cover and simmer for
5 minutes. Pour into a 1-1/2 quart casserole dish. Fold cheese
into mashed potatoes; spoon into a ring on top of meat. Bake,
uncovered, at 450 degrees for 15 minutes or until potatoes are
lightly browned on top. Makes 4 servings.

For a mock
shepherd's pie in
minutes, just
substitute a can of
cream of
celery soup
and frozen hash
browns for the
mashed potatoes...less
fuss and just as tasty!

# Garden Vegetable Casserole

1-1/2 c. rice, uncooked
5 tomatoes, sliced
3 zucchini, sliced
3 carrots, thinly sliced
2 green peppers, sliced into
  rings
1 onion, thinly sliced and
  separated into rings
3/4 c. water
6 T. olive oil
6 T. rice wine vinegar

3 T. fresh parsley, chopped
1 to 2 t. hot pepper sauce
2 cloves garlic, minced
1-1/2 t. salt
3/4 t. dried thyme
3/4 t. pepper
3/4 t. dried basil
1-1/2 c. shredded mozzarella
  cheese
1/3 c. grated Parmesan
  cheese

Place 3/4 cup rice in each of two, 11"x7" baking dishes. Layer half of vegetables over rice in each dish. In a small bowl, combine water, oil, vinegar, parsley, pepper sauce, garlic, salt, thyme, pepper and basil; stir until well blended. Pour half of oil mixture over vegetables in each dish. Bake, covered, at 350 degrees for 1-1/2 hours or until vegetables are tender. Sprinkle cheeses over both casseroles and continue to bake, uncovered, for approximately 10 minutes or until cheese melts. Each baking dish makes 6 to 8 servings.

This is a great casserole to whip up for a new mom or an elderly neighbor. Since the recipe makes 2 casseroles, keep one for dinner and hand-deliver the other!

## Calico Beans

1/2 lb. ground beef
1/2 lb. bacon, chopped
1 c. onion, chopped
1 clove garlic, minced
1/2 c. catsup
1 t. salt
1/4 c. brown sugar, packed
1 t. dry mustard

2 t. vinegar
16-oz. can lima beans,
   drained
2 16-oz. cans kidney beans,
   drained
3 16-oz. cans baked beans
   in sauce

Brown ground beef, bacon, onion and garlic together; drain.
Combine with remaining ingredients; bake, covered, at
350 degrees for 45 minutes, or use a slow cooker set on high
for 3 to 4 hours. Makes 12 servings.

A welcome
housewarming or
"get well soon"
gift...prepare a big
dish of Calico
Beans in a new
casserole dish and
enclose the recipe
along with a note
that says the dish
is theirs to keep!

## Country Potato Bake

1-lb. pkg. frozen hash
  browns
10-3/4 oz. can cream of
  chicken soup
1 c. sour cream
4 T. margarine, melted

1 c. shredded mild Cheddar
  cheese
6 slices bacon, crisply cooked
  and crumbled
2.8-oz. can French fried
  onions

Spread hash browns evenly in the bottom of a greased
13"x9" baking dish. Mix together soup, sour cream and
margarine; pour over hash browns. Sprinkle with cheese,
bacon and onions; bake, covered, at 350 degrees for
45 minutes. Makes 12 servings.

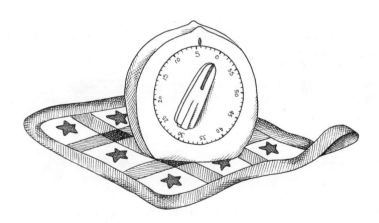

To keep casseroles from bubbling over, slip a toothpick
between the casserole dish and the lid...it'll allow steam
to escape and keep your oven clean!

## Corn Casserole

1/2 c. margarine, melted
14-3/4 oz. can creamed corn
2 eggs, beaten
1 c. Cheddar cheese, grated

1/2 c. cornmeal
1/2 t. onion salt
4-oz. can diced chilies
1 c. sour cream

Mix all ingredients together; bake, uncovered, in an
8"x8" baking dish at 350 degrees for 50 to 60 minutes. Makes
4 servings.

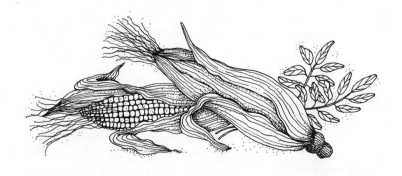

To freeze an extra casserole, just line the dish with
plastic wrap and spray with non-stick vegetable spray.
Add ingredients; fold plastic wrap over top and freeze.
When frozen, lift out and return the casserole to
freezer. To enjoy it later, remove the plastic wrap,
place casserole in original dish, thaw and bake.

# Ham & Noodle Casserole

1 onion, finely chopped
4 T. butter, melted
2 eggs, beaten
1 c. sour cream
1/2 c. shredded Swiss cheese

1-1/2 c. cooked ham,
   chopped
salt to taste
1/2 lb. egg noodles, cooked

Sauté onion in butter over medium heat until tender; set aside.
In a mixing bowl, combine eggs and sour cream; add onion
mixture, cheese and ham. Season with salt. Place noodles into
a buttered 2-quart casserole dish; add ham mixture and toss
gently. Bake, uncovered, at 350 degrees for 45 minutes or
until a knife inserted in the center comes out clean. Makes 6 to
8 servings.

Help potluck hosts keep track of dishes by taping
a label to the bottom of your casserole dish...
be sure to use a waterproof marker
and include your name and phone number.

## Cheesy Broccoli & Rice

10-3/4 oz. can cream of
   mushroom soup
10-3/4 oz. can cream of
   chicken soup
10-3/4 oz. can cream of
   celery soup
16-oz. jar pasteurized
   process cheese sauce

1/2 c. butter
16-oz. pkg. frozen, chopped
   broccoli
1 c. long-cooking rice,
   uncooked

Mix all ingredients together. Spread into a 13"x9" baking dish
coated with non-stick vegetable spray; bake, covered, at
325 degrees for 35 to 40 minutes, stirring after 20 minutes.
Makes 8 to 10 servings.

Need a handy recipe holder? Glue a cork to the top of
your recipe box, cut a slit across the top of the cork and
insert a recipe card.

# Ham & Cauliflower Au Gratin

2  10-oz. pkgs. frozen
    cauliflower, thawed
    and drained
1-1/4 c. smoked ham,
    cooked and chopped
10-3/4 oz. can condensed
    Cheddar cheese soup

1/4 c. milk
2/3 c. biscuit baking mix
2 T. butter
1/2 t. nutmeg
Garnish: fresh parsley,
    chopped and paprika

Arrange cauliflower in an ungreased 13"x9" baking dish; top
with ham. Blend soup and milk together in a mixing bowl until
smooth; pour over ham. Mix remaining ingredients until
crumbly; sprinkle over soup mixture. Bake, uncovered, at
400 degrees for 20 to 25 minutes or until topping is golden;
garnish with parsley and paprika before serving. Makes 12 to
15 servings.

To keep cauliflower fresh and creamy white,
add a tablespoon of milk to the water
when steaming or boiling.

## Chicken Casserole Supreme

3 whole chicken breasts
1 stalk celery, chopped
1/2 onion, chopped
salt & pepper to taste
2 c. sour cream
10-3/4 oz. can cream of
   mushroom soup

8-oz. pkg. herb-seasoned
   stuffing mix
1/2 c. butter, melted
1 c. chicken broth

Boil chicken breasts, celery, onion, salt and pepper together until chicken falls off bones and juices run clear. Cool until easy to handle, remove meat and cube. Combine chicken with sour cream and soup. Pour into a 2-quart casserole dish. In a mixing bowl, stir stuffing mix, butter and broth together; spread over chicken. Bake, uncovered, at 350 degrees for 45 minutes. Makes 6 to 8 servings.

Fill different size terra cotta pots with florist's foam,
then tuck in a bundle of wheat or rye. Tie a raffia bow
around the bundle and hide the foam with moss...
looks charming lined up on a buffet table!

# Turkey-Rice Casserole

10-3/4 oz. can cream of
   mushroom soup
10-3/4 oz. can cream of
   celery soup
1-1/2 c. milk

1-1/2 oz. pkg. dry onion
   soup mix
1 c. white rice, cooked
2 to 3 c. cooked turkey,
   cubed

Combine all ingredients in an ungreased 2-quart baking dish.
Bake, covered, at 350 degrees for 35 minutes; uncover, and
bake an additional 10 minutes. Makes 4 to 6 servings.

Gather some
friends and hold a
progressive
dinner where each
member of the
group fixes one
course of the meal...
everyone moves from
house-to-house for dinner. It's a great way to share
in the joy of home-cooking without all the fuss!

## Special Supper Stuffing

2 lbs. chicken breasts
2 1-lb. loaves white bread
1/2 c. fresh parsley, minced
1 c. onion, chopped
3/4 c. celery, chopped
1 c. carrot, shredded
1-1/4 c. boiled potatoes,
    finely chopped

1 T. fresh sage, chopped
1 t. fresh thyme, chopped
1 t. pepper
5 eggs
12-oz. can evaporated milk
2-1/2 c. chicken broth

Boil chicken breasts until tender and juices run clear when chicken is pierced. Set aside to cool slightly. Cube bread and toast on a baking sheet; transfer to a very large mixing bowl. Shred and chop chicken breasts; add to the bread cubes. Mix in the vegetables and seasonings; toss well. In a medium bowl, beat eggs, milk and broth; pour over the bread cube mixture, stirring gently. The mixture will be very moist. Allow to stand for one hour. Transfer stuffing to a greased 3-quart glass casserole dish; bake, uncovered at 350 degrees for 2 hours or until center puffs up and is golden brown. Serves 12 to 16.

Fill your kitchen windowbox with a miniature herb garden!
You can pinch off fresh sage, thyme, oregano or basil
whenever you need them for a yummy casserole.

# Autumn Red Potato Casserole

8 red potatoes
3 c. shredded mild Cheddar
    cheese
1/4 c. plus 2 T. butter

2 c. sour cream
1/3 c. green onions, chopped
1/4 t. salt
1 t. pepper

Boil potatoes until tender, but firm; cool, peel and dice. In a heavy saucepan, combine cheese and 1/4 cup butter over low heat; stir until cheese melts. Remove from heat; blend in sour cream, onions, salt and pepper. Gently fold into potatoes; transfer to a large casserole dish. Dot with remaining butter; bake at 350 degrees for 30 to 40 minutes. Makes 8 servings.

Drop a dryer sheet into soaking casserole
pans...baked-on crust comes off in an hour!

# Vegetable Lasagna

2 T. butter, melted
2 c. sliced mushrooms
1 onion, chopped
1 clove garlic, minced
2 T. all-purpose flour
1 t. pepper
1-1/4 c. milk
2  10-oz. pkgs. frozen,
  chopped spinach, thawed
  and drained
1 carrot, shredded

3/4 c. Parmesan cheese,
  shredded and divided
2 eggs, beaten
2 c. cottage cheese
2 c. ricotta cheese
1-1/2 t. Italian seasoning
10 lasagna noodles, cooked
  and drained
8-oz. pkg. mozzarella
  cheese, shredded, divided

Combine butter, mushrooms, onion and garlic in a skillet; sauté
until tender. Stir in flour and pepper; blend in milk, stirring well
until thick and bubbly. Cook and stir one minute more; remove
from heat. Add spinach, carrot and 1/2 cup of Parmesan
cheese; set aside. In a separate mixing bowl, combine eggs,
cottage cheese, ricotta cheese and Italian seasoning; set aside
In a greased 3-quart rectangular baking dish, layer the
following in order: 1/3 noodles, 1/3 cottage cheese mixture,
1/3 spinach mixture, 1/3 mozzarella cheese. Repeat the layers
2 more times; sprinkle with remaining Parmesan cheese. Bake,
uncovered, at 350 degrees for 35 minutes or until heated
through. Let stand 10 minutes before cutting. Makes 8 to
10 servings.

Place your onions in the freezer for 5 minutes before
slicing them...no more tears!

# Broccoli Casserole

16-oz. bag frozen chopped
  broccoli
10-oz. bag frozen chopped
  broccoli
2 10-oz. pkgs. chicken
  flavored rice-vermicelli
  mix

2 10-3/4 oz. cans cream of
  chicken soup
16-oz. pkg. pasteurized
  process cheese spread,
  cubed

Prepare broccoli and vermicelli according to package directions;
set aside. Spoon broccoli into a 4-qt. slow cooker; stir in soup.
Fold in cheese; mix well. Add vermicelli mix; heat until melted.
Makes about 32 servings.

Just making dinner for a few?
Divide the casserole ingredients into
two smaller dishes and freeze one for later
or share the extra with a friend or neighbor!

## Cheesy Macaroni & Beef

1 to 1-1/2 lbs. ground beef
14-oz. can stewed tomatoes,
   drained
26-oz. jar spaghetti sauce

2 7-1/4 oz. pkgs. macaroni
   and cheese, cooked
8-oz. pkg. shredded
   mozzarella cheese

In a large skillet, brown ground beef; drain. Add tomatoes and spaghetti sauce; stir in macaroni. Pour into an ungreased 13"x9" baking dish; sprinkle with cheese. Bake, uncovered, at 350 degrees for 20 minutes. Makes 4 to 6 servings.

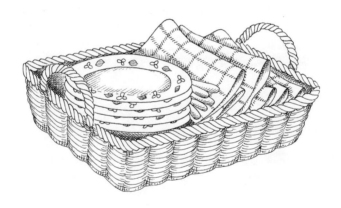

Host a family reunion this year!
Drape tables with old-fashioned quilts and
invite friends & family over to share
their favorite casseroles and comfort food.

# Stroganoff Casserole

8-oz. can sliced mushrooms
1 onion, chopped
3 cloves garlic, minced
1 t. oil
1/4 c. dry white wine
10-3/4 oz. can cream of
    mushroom soup

1/2 c. sour cream
1 T. Dijon mustard
1 lb. ground beef, browned
4 c. egg noodles, cooked
Garnish: fresh parsley,
    chopped

Sauté mushrooms, onion and garlic in oil until onion is tender; add wine. Reduce heat to medium; simmer for 3 minutes. Remove from heat; blend in soup, sour cream, mustard and ground beef. Spoon noodles into a lightly greased 13"x9" baking dish; pour beef and mushroom mixture over noodles, stirring to coat. Bake, uncovered, at 350 degrees for 30 minutes or until thoroughly heated; garnish with fresh parsley. Makes 6 servings.

Use our table tents for your signature casserole...
look for them on the very next page.
When your special dish is requested at the
next picnic, potluck or family reunion,
everyone in line will know just what's inside!

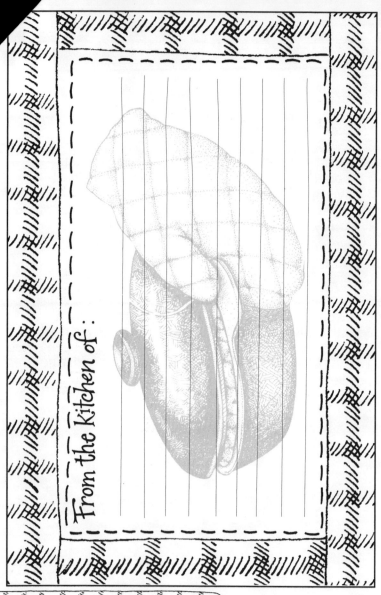

From the Kitchen of :

To:

From:

Pass a recipe along to a special friend with our casserole recipe card. Jus photocopy, cut and attach t home-cooked meals for guaranteed smiles.

Don't keep 'em guessing! Photocopy, cut out and write your recipe name on this card for a clever table tent. Just fold it in half and place it next to your dish at the next potluck.

# Index